Millionaire In

60 Minutes

7 **Surprising Things The Rich Do Differently**

Harvey Kinder

Table Of Content

INTRODUCTION:

The Millionaire Mindset

Do you know what differentiates the rich from the poor?

If you're under the impression that it's their bank balance, assets and materialistic and luxury belongings, you're wrong. What truly differentiate the two classes of people are their mindsets.

Their mental attitudes, behavioral traits and outlook on life bring about the vast disparities between the two. Are you amongst the people who are constantly struggling? Do you find yourself breaking your back on a monthly basis trying to make ends meet? Do you feel like you never have enough funds to do the things you dream of?

Well, then you're stuck with the mindset of the poor.

You need to understand that it isn't pure dumb luck that makes the rich wealthy. If you wish to be wealthy, successful and rich you need to change your mindset. Typically, the mindsets of the poor involve a lot of doubts, fears, sense of entitlements, grudges, blames, anger, jealousies, judgments, egos, and criticisms.

On the other hand, the behavioral traits of the rich involve gratitude, happiness for others, maintaining journals, discussing ideas, ready to learn attitudes, maintaining to-do lists, daily reading for self-improvement and setting and following goals. It doesn't matter if you're poor and unable to make ends meet if you want to shift your energies you need to change your mindset.

Millionaire In 60 Minutes is teach you the mindset, habits and work ethics of the rich along with step by step action plan that will mold you into the Super-Rich mindset.

You will find a **checklist, cheat-sheet and 21 Days habits program** which I warmly invite you to complete in order to maximize you results. It will help you understand your Goals, Purpose, and Reason to a greater extent making it easier to accomplish them.

You need to Analyze and start exhibiting the behavioral traits of the rich and lose the old set of beliefs that you clung to so dearly. Attempt this for just three months and witness the miraculous changes in your life. Now we will discuss the in-depth behavioral traits of the poor and how to change them.

Chapter 1

Pretending To Be Rich

A wise man once said, "We buy things we don't need with money we don't have to impress people we don't like." This is exactly the pattern that the poor are famous for following. Have you ever noticed how people who can barely make ends meet will go out of their way to purchase luxury items that are ridiculously expensive and absolutely unnecessary. They will max out their credit cards buying expensive watches, smartphones and branded fashion wear and find themselves in a quicksand of debt. Most people who are poor follow this nonsensical pattern repeatedly only to fool the world into believing that they are wealthy. They live a pretentious and fake life to impress the people around them and prove to society that they are financially very sound. Another reason why they do this is to boost their self-confidence and ego when they are amongst large crowds. The lack of funds and finances makes them so insecure about themselves that the temporary and fake sense of security that they find in pretending makes them happy.

Another costly mistake that the poor make is that they invest in depreciating assets such as expensive cars and end up in a financial position worse than they were in before. They try to live a life that is far above their means and just end up finding themselves in a financial mess that's nearly impossible to get out of. Living above their means increases the number of bills they have to pay every month; it makes it a big struggle for them to make ends meet. This pattern leads to diminished or zero savings, increased debts and not to forget constant stress and anxiety.

Impress or Invest?

Now let's discuss the behavioral traits of the rich. First and foremost, the rich don't pretend and they don't need to pretend because they just are. Contrary to popular belief that the rich live extravagant lifestyles and purchase luxury and unnecessary items, they don't. One excellent behavioral trait of the rich is that they live within their means. They buy what they can afford and don't go out of their way to prove their wealth. They buy the things that they need and not those that they want.

Another behavioral trait of the rich is that they invest their hard earned money wisely. You won't find the rich making nonsensical and impractical investment decisions and you will certainly not find them investing in depreciating assets like cars. The rich invest their money in appreciating assets such as land or gold. Investing in appreciating assets gradually increases their net worth and thereby increases their wealth. People who are rich are so extremely satisfied with themselves and their lives that they have no need whatsoever to spend money on unnecessary items. People who are constantly spending money on unnecessary items with the intention of flaunting them to the world only do so because somewhere deep down inside they are deeply dissatisfied with themselves and their lives.

Now that we have understood the basic difference between the behavioral traits of the rich and the poor, let's discuss certain changes you need to bring about in your mindset and your life in order to break out of that repeated pattern of poverty and constant struggling. Incorporating these changes in your life will help you shift your financial energies from negative to positive. Here's the list of changes you need to incorporate into your daily life:

First and foremost, you need to have gratitude. It doesn't matter if you have no money in your bank account or you haven't accomplished even half your goals. Have gratitude for every little and big thing in your life. Every time you get your monthly paycheck be grateful, be grateful for your family and friends, be grateful for the food you eat and just be grateful for everything that is going positive in your in your life.

"The weak can never forgive; forgiveness is the attribute of the strong." You need to learn how to forgive. In order to live the kind of lifestyle that the rich live, it is absolutely essential for you to forgive and let go. The rich don't hold on to anger and hurt and pain, they let it go. Holding onto any sort of negativity will only lead to negative circumstances in your life. So learn to forgive if you wish to grow in all aspects of your life.

Learn to respect and congratulate others when they are victorious. Don't hold on to grudges and jealousy.

In life, you're not always going to win. Sometimes you win and sometimes you lose. Learn to accept defeat with humility and take responsibility for your failures

Learn to compliment people on their achievements and successes. You won't become any lesser of a person if you shell out a few compliments every now and then

Make it a point to read a little bit every single day. By reading we don't mean romance novels and comic books. By reading, we mean that you should read self-improvement books, read about various cultures, read material that will help you grow as a human being

Keeping a journal is another very important thing to do if you want to become rich. A large number of rich and successful people have been known to maintain journals. Not only do journal entries help you heal but they also boost your confidence and help you assist you in achieving your goals.

Don't be afraid to openly discuss ideas that cross your mind. Discussing your ideas with others will quickly and efficiently help you improvise on them and incorporate them faster

Ensure that you maintain a daily to-do list. Not only do you need to maintain the list but ensure that you get all the work done on time. Rich people always keep and follow their to-do lists

The only thing in life that's certain is change. So don't be afraid to embrace change. Let it happen. Change is essential for you to grow spiritually, mentally and emotionally. The rich are open and welcoming to change

Bringing about these changes in your life and changing your mindset will sincerely help you in making the transition from poor to rich. So stop pretending to be something you're not, stop wasting money on unnecessary products and stop trying to impress people who don't even matter. Work on changing your behavioral traits and start incorporating the habits of the rich.

Chapter 2

Become The Employer

Most people who are struggling to make ends meet or are constantly in a financial soup are the people who have jobs. They are working night and day just to climb higher up on the corporate ladder. They are part of the rat race that just ends up leaving them exhausted and dissatisfied with their lives. The rich on the other hand are the ones who own the businesses. The rich are on top of the corporate ladder that the poor are desperately trying to ascend. Are you completely and utterly fed up and exhausted with being part of the rat race? If your answer is yes, then you need to start incorporating some changes in your daily routine. We will now discuss what it is you can do to break out of the rat race.

5 Step To Become The Employer

Step 1 Decide- **Make A Firm Decision That You Want Out:** The first step to breaking out of the rat race is deciding that you want to. You need to understand that you may slog all through your life but still not be able to pay off your debts or even save money for the future. It doesn't matter how many hours you put in, it doesn't matter if you break your back working, there are certain benefits that your own business can give you that a job never will.

"If you don't build your dream, someone else will hire you to to help them build theirs."

You don't need to stay back at a job that you absolutely despise. There are millions of people out there just like you who stick on with jobs they hate and keep putting away their dreams for tomorrow. By the time they are ready to focus on accomplishing their desires it's too late. So decide now whether or not you want to break out of the rat race. Once you have made a concrete decision, the steps that follow are simple and easy.

Step 2 Quit Your Job— **Breaking Out Of The Rat Race:** Once you have decided that you wish to break out of the rat race, the next step is to set up your very own business. It doesn't necessarily need to be a business that involves large investments; it can be a small time online business or a business that you commence from your home. Do keep in mind that when you're setting up your very own business, a large number of people including family and friends will try to talk you out of doing so. They will highlight the negative points of setting up the business and may try to break your confidence. At this point, if you break and chicken out, you're going to be stuck playing the role of an employee for the rest of your life. We aren't saying that there aren't risks in setting up your own business. You may excel or you may fail. But the point here is that you need to try. Like a wise man once said, "In order to succeed you must first be willing to experience failure." It doesn't matter if you fail a few times before success finds you, just don't forget to overcome your fear of failure if you truly wish to move forward and break out of the awful rat race.

Step 3 Start-up- **Start Off As A Part Time Entrepreneur:** Now when we say that set up your own business that does not mean you instantly quit your job and simply focus on starting up your business. You need to handle this step practically and in a way that will be beneficial for you and not detrimental. Now you're probably thinking that you won't have the time to continue your job and set up your own business simultaneously. Well, don't say you don't have time, you have the exact number of hours a day Albert Einstein had. You don't need to spend 40 hours a week trying to set up your own business. Initially, while starting off you can invest about 10 to 15 hours a week. That is around 1.5 to 2 hours a day and you can definitely find that minimal amount of time in your daily schedule. Turn off from all distractions and sincerely focus on the set up of your business, this is sure shot bet for you to be able to break out from the rat race.

Step 4 Budget– Limit Your Expenditure: Setting up your own business will require you to limit your expenditure and keep unnecessary costs at bay. With advancing technology, the need for you to maintain and pay the rent of a warehouse to store goods is diminishing; this ends up resulting in a significant amount of savings. Besides this, you need to also limit your personal expenditure. You need not spend money on unnecessary luxury items, clothes, shoes and other products. If you're used to visiting a pub every night for a drink or two, cut down on that as well. You probably don't realize that reducing certain personal and unnecessary monthly costs result in a large amount of savings. All the money you save can be redirected into the business expenses.

Step 5 Believe– Stay Focused: You may initially find it very hard to stay focused on setting up your business. You may not be able to manage your time in an appropriate manner and you will struggle with juggling multiple things at once. But whatever you do, don't lose focus. Stay dedicated to your cause and keep on reminding yourself that it is only the beginning stages of this change that will keep you stressed out. Once you get used to the routine and your mind and body get attuned to the changes, things will be a lot smoother.

These steps will gradually help you break out of the rat race that you're stuck in and help you move forward in life. Another thing that you need to understand if you wish to become rich and successful is the power of passive income. The rich understand the power of passive income and how important a role it plays in financial progress. Let's not understand what passive income really means. In lay man's terms, a passive income is nothing but a regular income that is generated without any efforts. Some examples of passive income include various types of property incomes, royalties, interest from your bank account and so on. Find a way to earn passive income yourself. It can be through leasing out an extra apartment that you have or through royalties for a book or song you wrote. Earning passive income will keep you stress-free and give you a source of additional income. So just like the rich, understand the power and necessity of a passive income if you truly wish to shift your financial energies.

All in all, you need to stop focusing all your energy on trying to ascend the corporate ladder. On the other hand, redirect your focus to breaking out of the rat race and setting up your very own business.

Chapter 3

Paycheck VS Passive Income

Have you ever noticed how the poor pretty much live pay check to paycheck month after month? They have no other source of income besides their salary check. Every month the income that comes through the salary check is spent on making ends meet, basic necessities, bills, and other expenses and eventually they are left with virtually no savings whatsoever. Although they are well aware of this pattern, they still hold on to it with their dear lives. Let's now discuss what it is that prevent the poor from breaking out of this pattern.

Most people are so terrified of breaking out of their comfort zone that they prefer to live in an environment that's safe and secure rather than one that involves taking risks. Their jobs and monthly paychecks give them a sense of security and comfort. Having a fixed job doesn't involve any kind of risk that will result in loss of money. So they rather live pay check to paycheck, even if that means barely making ends meet on a monthly basis. The rich on the other hand are not afraid to take calculated risks. They have the courage to break out of their comfort zones and don't depend on a fixed monthly source of income. The rich also understand that failure is the stepping stone to success and are not afraid of failing a few times before success finds them. So if you really want to live the kind of lifestyle that the rich live, the first thing you need to do is break out of your comfort zone and start taking risks in your life.

Save To Build: The first step to breaking out of the pay check to pay check living pattern is to start saving money only with an intention to build your business with what you've saved. You may be thinking that it's not possible for you to save any money because all the money you receive in your monthly paycheck goes towards paying your bills and other expenses. But the point here is that you don't need to save half of paycheck every month. If you can keep aside 15 to 20 percent of your paycheck on a monthly basis, which is good enough. Repeatedly saving every month will gradually help you have enough savings for you to start your company or a small business for sure.

Spend Wisely: Stop wasting money on unnecessary items. You probably don't realize it but there may be at least a dozen things that you purchase on a daily or monthly basis that are absolutely unnecessary and a complete waste of money. It doesn't matter if it's a cup of coffee, chewing gum or even bottled water, it's time you started thinking twice before spending money on unnecessary items. To make it easier for you to understand the kind of money you spend on unnecessary items start keeping a little notebook on all the money you have spent for a couple of weeks. This exercise will truly throw some light on your spending patterns. Reducing such expenditures will definitely give you some additional savings at the end of the month.

Hustle: Work as much as you can. Well as we all know it, the global economy is in a catastrophic state and personal financial matters are going to be troublesome until the world economy doesn't stabilize. If the company you are working for offers paid overtime, it's time you start making the most of it. Besides this, another way of making some additional income is by taking up a second job or a part-time job that pays well. Although initially, it may seem like a tough job to handle two jobs simultaneously, push yourself as much as you can to juggle both. You won't realize it immediately but that additional money can really help you in the long run and often proves to be extremely handy. Following this step will also gradually help you break out of the pattern of living pay check to pay check and reduce your struggle of making ends meet.

Budget: If you really wish to break out of the pay check to pay check living pattern, draw up a budget for yourself and stick to it. Sticking to your budget on a monthly basis will result in you saving lots of money and can gradually help you break out of the pattern of struggling to make ends meet every month.

No debt: Get rid of that credit card. A wise man once said, "Use your credit card for convenience and not for credit." A lot of people end up maxing out their credit cards purchasing items that are absolutely unnecessary. If you're living a life that is completely dependent on your monthly paycheck, then owning a credit card is a miserable idea. Constant and repeated use of a credit card will only increase your debt and worsen your financial situation. Get rid of all those credit cards as soon as you can and any pending debts that are owed by you to the credit card company must be paid off in a systematic manner at the earliest.

Invest: Stop buying things you don't need. Each and every one of us tends to waste money every now and then on things we don't need. If you really want to break out of your paycheck to paycheck living pattern it's about time that you start purchasing the things you need and not the things you want. Look around your home, you are guaranteed to find a ton of things that you purchased that are absolutely unnecessary and a complete waste of money. It's time you stopped spending money on junk and start saving that money for business investment.

No Loan: Don't take loans or borrow money for luxury. Taking a loan for personal expense is the worst thing you can ever do. It will gradually worsen your financial situation and paying the ridiculous interest amounts will cut you in half. Even borrowing money from friends or from family is a bad idea. Even if they aren't charging you interest, it only increases your debt and increases the chances of ruining your relationship with the person giving the loan. So under no circumstances should you be taking a loan of any sort of you wish to break out of the pattern of living pay check to pay check.

If you really go to see, the rich aren't dependent on their paychecks. They have made so many wise investment decisions and also receive remuneration from various sources of passive income. They aren't concentrating on making ends meet every month, on the contrary, they have enough money to spend and saved as well. If you really want to live the kind of life the rich live it's time for you to start taking risks and chances. You need to be willing to lose a little in order to gain a lot. You need to break out of your comfort zone and stop depending on the security and stability of your underpaid job. What you don't realise is that there is only so much a person can grow when working for someone, on the other hand, if you are running your own business and taking certain calculated risks, your financial growth will also become unlimited.

Chapter 4

Money While You Sleep

You need to stop working for money and start making the money work for you instead. The poor are famous for exchanging their precious time and sincere efforts for money. They work hard all day, everyday to earn money that will pay their monthly bills and expenses. The first thing the poor need to understand is that in order to become rich, they need to work smart, not hard. You don't see the rich spending each waking hour of the day working to make money. You need to be practical about making money and ensure that the money you make is utilized in a way to attract more money. Now let's discuss how we can make money work for you and not the other way around.

How To Invest

Start Building Assets: The only way the rich get richer is because they have assets that work for them. It is necessary to develop a mindset of having multiple sources of income wherein you have revenue coming in from different investments you've made. You can learn more about this in my Book Passive Income: Passive Income:5 Proven Methods & Mind-sets to Make 500-10000 a month in 45 days

Get Yourself A Savings Account With A High Yield: The first and most important way to make your money work for you is by investing a decent chunk of it in a savings bank account that offers a high rate of interest. You need to keep aside at least 6 months' worth of your monthly earnings in this account for best results. Investing your funds in a financial institution that offers an excellent rate of interest will help in generating additional value to your funds while they sit around in your account. If you're uncertain about what banking or financial institution can provide you such services, speak to your financial advisor and get proper guidance from him.

Put Your Funds Away In Your Retirement Account: If you start putting a certain amount of your monthly earnings into a retirement account, it will really make your money work for you. Retirement accounts are taxed at a much lower rate and regular savings in your retirement account can really help you in the future.

Invest In The Stock Market: Now by investing we don't mean risky trading but we mean long-term investing. Save a chunk of your money and invest it in the stock market. Ensure that you stay invested in the stocks you purchase for at least over a year, this way you can avoid paying capital gains tax and can maximize the return on your investment.

Buy Gold: Gold is an ever-appreciating asset that proves to be an excellent investment. Take a chunk of your savings and invest it in physical gold that you can store away in the bank vault. Another great advantage of investing in gold is that you will get immediate cash if you ever wish to sell it in the future due to unforeseen circumstances. So keep accumulating gold every chance you get if you really want to make your money work for you.

Invest In Real Estate: Just like gold even real estate is an ever-appreciating asset. Like Mark Twain once said, "Buy land, they're not making it anymore." Investing in real estate can be doubly beneficial to you. For one, it will give you excellent returns and secondly you can always lease out the apartment or plot that you buy and get an additional source of income through the rent. Investment in real estate is a wonderful way of getting your money to work for you.

The rich exactly follow the above-mentioned pattern. They invest in appreciating assets that increase their overall net worth. You won't find the rich working for money; they do whatever it takes to make their money work for them. The beauty of the investments that the rich make is that their investments make them earn money even while they are sleeping. Wouldn't it be wonderful if you too could earn money while you were sleeping? Wouldn't it be an excellent feeling if you didn't have to work everyday, all day to make money? It is now possible for you also to live the lifestyle of the rich. But in order to do so, you first need to break out of your comfort zone. Let's now discuss how to break out of the security of your comfort zone so that you can stop working for money and start making money work for you:

Do something different everyday. It doesn't necessarily need to be a huge change that will take your life by storm. It can be something very basic and small like taking a different route to the gym or eating breakfast for dinner. Following this step will help you in recalibrating your sense of reality and thus gradually help you break out of the dependency that you have on your job and break the false sense of security that you get from your job.

Slow down a little bit when making decisions. Most of us live such fast paced and hectic lives that we don't really think we just do. You're so consumed with the fact that you need to work hard and focus all of your energy on work that you actually forget to give yourself a little bit of time to think before making personal or other important decisions. So slow down, think before you act, give yourself the time to understand what is going on around you and react and make decisions in a way that's in your best interest.

It is absolutely essential for you to be impulsive every once in a way. Most of the time you're so conditioned and comfortable with your work routine, that you base your decisions in accordance to work. When was the last time you just took off for a small vacation or took a day off from work to spend it with your family and loved ones? It's ok to be impulsive and not let your entire life revolve around your work.

Now we aren't saying that you need to make drastic and dramatic changes in your life overnight. It is understandable that for someone whose entire life revolves around working for money, making changes can be extremely difficult. So you don't need to directly take the plunge all at once. You can take baby steps to make changes in your life that will gradually break you out of your comfort zone and help you stop working for money and start making your money work for you.

So if you really wish to live the kind of life the rich live, start behaving like the rich. Invest in appreciating assets, stop letting your life revolve around your work, let your wise investments make the money for you and most importantly stop working for money.

You can find out about more methods to earn money online in my book

Passive Income:5 Proven Methods & Mind-sets to Make 500-10000 a month in 45 days

Chapter 5

Importance Of Written Goals

"Have goal so big, you get uncomfortable telling them to small minded people"

Another very important behavioral trait of the rich is that they always write down their goals. The poor on the other hand never ever write down their goals and objectives. The poor are so terrified of setting big goals that they never ever really come around to writing them down. They lack the self-confidence that is required in order to achieve goals. They always undermine and undervalue their capabilities and talents and go about living a life that is nothing more than mediocre. They are under the false impression that life cannot be controlled and it is life that controls you. The poor are victims of circumstances and never take on the responsibility of changing their life around. The rich on the other hand have such big goals and ambitions that they actually put in efforts to change their lives around. We will now discuss the advantages of writing down your goals and how it will help you prosper.

6 Reasons You Should Set Goals

Clarity

It will give you clarity on what you should do next. One of the most important advantages of goal writing is that it will give you clarity on what your next step in life and business should be. People who have no written goals tend to go about life like aimless wanderers. If you don't know what your final destination is, how will you know what road to take? Thus writing down your goals is absolutely essential. They are the perfect way for you to stay focused and move forward in life with purpose. So start writing down your goals and more importantly stick to them if you wish to be successful and rich.

Reason

Gives you a reason to wake up in the morning. If you don't have goals in life, what is it that you wake up for in the morning? Writing down your goals will give you a reason to wake up every morning and start your day with enthusiasm and excitement. You're not a robot, you're human. You need motivation, you need a purpose, and you need something that gives you an adrenaline rush. Writing down your goals does exactly that. It gives you something to look forward to, it gives you things to work towards and most importantly it gives you a reason to get out of bed every morning.

Focus

Keeps you focused and on track. Imagine if you had to go visit a friend who lived in a small village around 100 miles away from your home, but you didn't have your friend's address. You weren't just going to start your car and drive around aimlessly for 100 miles in hopes that you may stumble upon your friend's home. Not having your goals written down is like not having your friends address and hoping that some wonderful stroke of luck will just get you to your destination. Writing down your goals keeps you on track, tells you exactly what road you need to take in order to reach your destination. Writing your goals down allows you to keep your focus on the right road and gets you there on time and smoothly.

Progress

Becomes easier for you to keep track of your progress. If you don't know where you have to reach, how will you know how far along you are? Writing down your goals helps you to keep track of your progress. It makes you realise how well you're performing and how quickly you're moving closer to achieving the things that you want. It is essential to keep track of your progress. It helps you to understand when you're slacking and that you need to buck up in order to achieve your goals faster.

Motivation

Written down goals motivate you to work harder and more sincerely. They serve as a constant reminder that you need to be performing your best in order to achieve your goals. So write down your goals and read them daily, they will give you that push you constantly require to remain motivated.

Success

The chances of achieving your written goals are much higher. Writing down your goals increase your chances of achieving them. Typically, you will have three types of goals, your long term goals, your medium term goals and your short term goals. Writing down these goals will help you begin with your short term goals and gradually place yourself in a way that you work towards achieving your long term goals.

Understand that writing down your goals will help you become richer faster. It will efficiently shift your financial energies from negative to positive. Don't be afraid to dream big or to have goals that are of an intimidating size. It is your fear of dreaming big to prevent you from achieving the things you really desire. The rich on the other hand are fearless when it comes to dreaming big. They make plans and set targets that seem nearly impossible to achieve to most people. As Bo Jackson once said, "Set your goals high and don't stop until you get there." This is exactly what the rich do. They keep themselves focused and avoid taking their eyes off the goal. They move forward meandering around the obstacles that they encounter on the way with the ultimate intention of reaching their final destination. Follow these patterns of the rich, you have the exact same blood running through your veins as they do and it is equally possible for you to achieve your goals and break out of your financial negativity.

There maybe a feeling or a thought inside of you that constantly tells you that you will never be able to achieve exceptionally large goals in life. These thoughts probably occur in your mind because all through your life your parents, teachers, peers, friends and family members have always told you to be practical and avoid dreaming too big as it will only lead to disappointments. What if we told you that all these people were wrong? Find it hard to believe? Think about the quality of life these people who have discouraged you from dreaming big live.

Are they rich and successful and do they live a fulfilling life or are they living mediocre and ordinary lives? It is most likely that they live miserably mediocre lives that provide them a false sense of security. Don't blame them for guiding you the wrong way all their lives. This is exactly what they were taught to do and that's all that they know. Their minds have been conditioned in that way and they encourage you to believe the same. But it's now finally time for you to break out of those chains. It's time for you to start thinking, writing and achieving your goals. A major shift in your financial energies are along the way, just live and think like the rich and break out of those old patterns that you are used to following.

Chapter 6

Work Like A Millionaire

A Rich person knows the reality of life but chooses to focus his or her energy on the brighter side. It is a choice between a half-full and a half-empty glass—a matter of disposition or way of thinking.

The next steps that you will read are not a walk in a park, especially at first; but you can definitely do it! The more that you exercise the Millionaire mindset, the more it will be a part of your system. It is a conscious decision that you will go through every day, but nothing else will yield to a better result in your life. Actress Patricia Neal said, "A strong, positive mental attitude will create more miracles than any wonder drug." This pertains not only to the physical aspect but also to the mental, social and psychological aspect.

16 Tips For Super-Rich Mindset

Tip #1: Evaluate yourself (honestly) – You can do this by meditating or having a quiet me-time. You have to identify your usual negative thoughts and from they come. You have to be specific on what area of your life is most affected by your negative thinking. Is it about the way you look, your work, or your romantic relationship? Once it is identified, you have to again reflect and think if beating yourself up or thinking negatively about the situation will help dispel any issues. Ask yourself if your negative thoughts are helping to better the situation. If your answer is no, then the next step is crucial. You have to think of a way to change the situation. Positive thinking calls for an action, not just simply giving up wallowing in a situation. As you begin to practice necessary actions, you will most likely see the results and be inspired to move forward.

It is not a matter of developing an ego, but it is believing that you can further improve yourself and attain whatever you put your mind to.

Tip #2: Squash the negative small voices – With this, you have to be in tune with your thoughts and emotions. When you start to hear your inner voice that tells you that you are not good enough and will not succeed, you have to catch yourself and again meditate and find the positive view of the situation. Another technique is to develop positive statements to replace the negative thoughts that you are entertaining. Change your "I can't" to "I will". Erase words like stress, anger, depression, jealousy, etc. and lean more toward happy, peaceful, loving, motivated, etc. Do not forget that your thoughts become words and actions.

Remember that this is about choices and a matter of self-control. Do not give in to the voice that wants you to be hopeless, helpless and stressed-out. You know that you can do it. You just have to be proactive in dealing with life's challenges.

Tip #3: Ask for help –It is never bad to ask for help from your loved-ones or to seek professional help, especially if you are experiencing major breakdowns, insecurities and other negative emotions that are leading you to self-destruct. A professional can also help you find out the origin of your actions or negative thoughts and, at the same time, can direct you towards healing your heart and mind. Yes, change will start with you, but sometimes, recognizing that you have a problem, knowing its magnitude and sharing it with other people that you trust can definitely help you. There are times that what we need is just reassurance from another person to make things better.

Tip #4: Practice self-affirmation- While we usually want to hear affirmations from other people and even define oneself with their comments or views about us, we have to be grounded in the sense that we know who we really are and, of course, in our self-worth.

Sometimes we also have to say "I can do it! I can do this!" -- Even when you don't really believe that you can, by repeatedly saying it with conviction, you will soon realize that you really can do it. Have your own "magic" statement or a mantra. It can "trick" your mind to actually believe in it. Repeat it over and over, or you can also write the positive thought or say it out loud.

Tip # 5: Be at your best always - Giving your best shot will make you feel good about yourself and, at the same time, you are giving your self-esteem a healthy boost. For example, you have a presentation at your office. It may be part of your regular meeting only. However, by delivering a presentation wherein you have done your best, not only will you be confident with your work, but other people will surely notice it. Don't be surprised if you receive good feedback (write it down!) and that, in turn, will add more to your confidence level.

Tip #6: Move your body! – Moving your body like exercising and engaging in physical activities can improve your mood. Exercise will not only make your body healthy, but it will also help your mind and emotions to function better. In addition, exercises like yoga can also help release negative energies inside us. They will clear our mind and give us additional strength to face any trials that may come our way. You should couple exercise with healthy food and proper nutrition.

Tip #7: Develop a sense of gratitude - This is a must for everyone if you want to change your perspective into a healthier one. You have to learn to fully recognize and appreciate the good things in life. Why? Your sense of gratitude will feed your feelings of satisfaction and increase your optimism. Why choose to be sad, depressed or agitated when you have all the things in life that you can be thankful for?

Let's try this simple exercise. Develop your "list of gratitude." Just jot down everything in life that can bring you happiness, or the things that you appreciate (even simple things like the beautiful sky that looks like a perfect canvass). Continue adding to the list. At the end of the exercise, you will surely realize that life is good and pessimistic ideas should have no room in your thoughts.

Tip #8: Face the reality that you are not perfect, but can be a better version of yourself - You have to know and understand that no matter how great you are, how stable your life may seem, there will be times that you will have to face problems that can make you fall apart. But the important thing here is that you also know that if you "survive" this phase, then you will come out to be a better version of yourself. So you have to hold on, think of a solution and be patient. This is also closely connected to developing your self-esteem, wherein you will push yourself to achieve your maximum potential.

Tip #9: Do not be too hard on yourself – Sometimes, we are our own worst critics, so you have to work on that. Our self-criticism can cause the flow of negative thoughts and even be the reason for our breakdowns. You have to celebrate every small victories and achievement, and if faced with problems, make sure that your assessment of the situation is not exaggerated or based on emotional thinking.

Instead of saying, "I studied my lessons, but I think I will still fail," say "Let's see what happens when I do my best and what I can do for my next step." Or "I may not be good at this, but with practice, I can do so much better."

Clean up your negative statements and learn to refocus. Do not be too hard yourself. You should be your self's biggest fan.

Tip #10: Don't always take things personally – This is one of the characteristics of a negative thinker: automatically blaming oneself for bad things that are happening and be frustrated and depressed by them. Reality check: The world is not all about you. You have to understand that you cannot control how others may think or act, but you can control yourself. You also have to accept other people's individuality that dictates their actions. Instead of getting easily frustrated, try to be in other people's shoes or think of possible reasons for their actions instead of flatly blaming yourself.

Tip #11: Choose rational thinking over emotional reasoning – Closely related to not taking things personally, you have to undo the habit of emotional reasoning as this is highly illogical and will make you feel worse. In every situation, you have to think things through before reacting to them. Do not base your belief on feelings alone.

One should also be more factual in dealing with stressful events or accept the reality, but at the same time look for a solution. For example, "The event that I handled could have been better, but it is not that bad," followed by "Next time I plan to do this...so that it will be successful." By doing this, you are choosing to learn from your mistakes, instead of irrational reasoning that will only further put yourself down. Another golden lesson for this is that there are times that we simply have to accept the things that we cannot change, shut down the negative thinking and move on.

Another trait to learn in order not to be overwhelmed with emotional reasoning is to be a determinist. This means that you understand that a behaviour or experience has a cause and effect and not just because of irrational or gut feelings. For example, you feel that you will have a bad day, but there is no logical reason behind it, it may be just triggered by a bad incident earlier in your day. Erase the thought immediately and don't let that thought define your day.

Tip #12: Turn your "what ifs" into actions – You have to learn to face your fears. For example, you fear that you may lose your job, you may entertain your worst-case scenario, but again, you have to be proactive and think of a solution if it happens, or how to prevent it from happening by reinventing yourself. Let go of the fear, as it may cripple you. You may not notice this, but sometimes, your fear is acting out, your anxiety is showing and, in effect, you are not working the way that you should be and will indeed lose the job in the long run.

If you have lost your job, then remember that our failures do not define us, but what defines us is the way we stand, face our obstacles and have a better version of ourselves.

Tip # 13: Stop over thinking – It is easy to be caught up with our fast-paced existence but do not forget the essentials in your life. Remind yourself of the things that are valuable. Always think positively and enjoy life's precious moments and again, do not over think. Give yourself a breather. Have a goal, but do not waste your time worrying about uncertain things. Instead, rejoice over the littlest triumphs and learn from every mistake.

Tip # 14: Learn to be open to change- Sometimes our negative thoughts stem from not being open to change. Instead of welcoming and facing the changes in our lives, we react by fearing the unknown. What we do not understand is that we should take what we can get with every new situation. It is normal and okay to feel a little fear or discomfort, but if you let that fear to get the best of you and control you, then you are keeping yourself from growing, evolving, and reaching your potential. Change is inevitable, but you are also designed to cope with change. It is just a matter of mindset.

Tip # 15: Give yourself a break–Sometimes, when a situation is so heavy that you can't think clearly, and then you need to "walk away" from the mess and take a break. By allowing yourself actually to loosen up and enjoy the things in life in a different setting, you are basically helping yourself to de-stress and to reset your mindset, so that when you are finally ready, you have a fresher and clearer mind to combat life's obstacles.

But take note that even if you are not facing a particular problem, it is a must that you reward yourself from time to time. Spend a day doing the things that make you happy, or spend some quality time with your family and friends. Aside from the fact that you deserve a good break, think of it as a way to fill up your "positivity" container, so that when problems arise or depressions set in, you also have happier thoughts to get you through the day or simply inspire you. It may seem odd but nature is one of the best therapists. Being out in nature has wonderful effects on your physical and mental well-being. We live in a world that's slowly tipping over the robotic and that's just harmful and detrimental for our overall well being. It has been scientifically proven that spending time in nature can boost your immunity levels, ground you, improve your psychological health and recalibrate your biological clock. So find some time in your daily schedule to go out for a walk on the beach or spend some time in the park or even just go for a stroll in the woods.

Tip # 16: Change your mental filter- "When life gives you lemons, make lemonade." This is about the power of changing how we view things. Our minds have a filter, and our habits usually determine how we react to things. How do you transform your mental filter? Here's an example: You are running late and stuck in traffic. Your pessimistic self will most likely start to panic and negative thoughts will run down your mind. This may be hard, but how about accepting the fact that you do not have control over the situation? Why not take the opportunity to chat with your partner? Read an e-book, fix your makeup or pray? Another example: You are in a stressful situation; in which you feel that you are close to a breaking point. Change your mental filter and see that you also have the inner strength to combat the situation, that you have friends or colleagues that will help you through the trying times.

Important Habits To Consider

Invest wisely: It's a very sad and bitter truth but the only investments that the poor make involve investments in materialistic products and unnecessary things like television and social media websites. You don't ever find the poor investing in themselves. The rich, on the other hand, ensure that they invest time in themselves. The rich focus on mental, spiritual and emotional improvement. They set aside a few hours a day in their schedule to focus on themselves. If you really wish to live the life of the rich and successful, you need to stop wasting your time on trivial and unnecessary things and start paying more attention to yourself. Now we will discuss what you need to do in order to invest time in yourself.

Live Within Your Means Initially: The first and most important habit you need to focus on is living within your means. Now you may be the kind of person who goes out of your way to purchase luxury goods and products just to flaunt them to the world. Well here's a little reality check for you; you don't have to prove anything to anyone. It doesn't matter what car you drive or what brands you sport or how big your house is, what really matters is whether or not you're living a life that makes you happy and gives you a sense of fulfilment. Stop maxing out credit cards to buy things you don't need, instead focusing on self-improvisation and always remember that in the end, everyone's outcome is the same and the only things that you will ever have are the memories and the stories to tell. So live within your means and live a life that's beautiful, fulfilling and emotionally and spiritually satisfying.

Read on a Daily Basis: Reading is essential for self-improvement. Now by reading, we don't mean you need to read comic books and mystery novels. You need to read self-improvement books, books about the human mind, psychology and different cultures. Read articles on statistics, self-improvement, general knowledge, spiritual articles and so on. Such material will help you grow on a spiritual, mental and emotional level. It will teach you to handle situations and circumstances in life much better. Like a wise man once said, "Reading gives us somewhere to go when we have to stay where we are." Reading will increase your imaginative powers, it will give you ideas that you can incorporate into your daily life and most importantly it will increase your knowledge. Thus, if you truly want to spend some time on yourself, inculcate the habit of reading. For those of you who aren't comfortable reading, you can also listen to audiobooks for similar effects. Audio books are a great option as well.

Meditate For Peace: In order to be successful one must meditate. The fast paced lives we live, leave our minds confused and scattered. Our concentration powers are slowly diminishing and our dependency on electronic gadgets and other equipment are increasing.

Meditation has a way of bringing you back to peace. It calms your mind and allows your confused mind to focus. Meditation pulls you back together. Find time every morning to meditate for at least ten minutes. Switch off your phone, get rid of all distractions and simply focus on your breath. Every time you find your mind wandering away, bring your focus back to your breath. As St. Francis De Sales once said, "When there is peace and meditation, there is neither anxiety nor doubt."

Exercise: No matter who you are or how busy you are, find time in the day to exercise. Exercise has a magical way of revitalizing the mind, body and soul. An hour long cardio session will not only energize you but it will give you the motivation you need to accomplish your goals of the day. The rich find the time in the day to exercise and if you wish to be like them so should you.

Eat Quality, Don't Be Cheap: You must have heard the famous saying, "You are what you eat." In order to be successful and rich, you need to eat healthy. It may seem like the two have no connection but in reality, they do. Eating healthy keeps your mind and body well nourished. A well-nourished mind gets better ideas and can work more effectively and maximize productivity. You cannot be healthy and energized by eating French fries and stuffing burgers. A well-nourished body does not tire or get exhausted easily and will allow you to work long hours without aches and pains. So do yourself a favor and get rid of those cookie boxes from your kitchen counter and replace your unhealthy and junk snacks with fruits, nuts, and berries.

So find some time in your day and invest that time wisely in yourself. This is the surest and fastest way to overall growth. No matter how busy the wealthy may be, they find time for themselves and make the most of it. If you wish to shift your financial energies from negative to positive, you too should invest some time in yourself.

Chapter 7

Willing To Sacrifices

In order to gain something, you have to be willing to lose something as well. If you're stuck making ends meet, you're probably not willingly taking any risks either. You're stuck in your comfort zone and refuse to break out of it. You're so used to your routine that disrupting your routine sounds ridiculous and seems impossible. Making sacrifices is just something that the poor don't know or comprehend. The rich on the other hand are ready to make sacrifices and they are ready to break out of their comfort zone. The rich are ready to tolerate certain discomforts in order to achieve their goals. Now we will discuss certain sacrifices that you need to make in order to live the kind of life that the rich live.

8 Sacrifices You'll Have To Make

Time: Don't say you don't have time; you have the exact number of hours a day Albert Einstein had. One of the things you need to sacrifice in order to achieve your goals is your time. You need to give time to things that are more important and things that bring you closer to your final destination and give up things that are simply a waste of time. For instance, if you enjoy partying every other night, you need to gradually reduce the number of times a week you get out to party and indulge in socializing and spend that time wisely towards increasing the work load you take up or completing certain tasks that you have pending and so on. Partying and indulging in alcohol is not really going to get you closer to achieving your goals. Investing your time wisely in sensible and productive activities will help you in the long run.

Stability: Often in order to become rich, the one thing you need to sacrifice is a stable life. A stable life comprises of a fixed job, fixed source of monthly income and the living a pay check to paycheck lifestyle. Sometimes following your goals and dreams require you to sacrifice the stability in your life and embrace a certain amount of unpredictability. Although it may sound strange but if you truly wish to grow as a person and break out of your comfort zone, you need to be willing to take certain risks in your life.

Personal Life: Following your dreams and achieving your goals often requires you to sacrifice a certain amount of your personal life. Often you may not be able to show up at a family function, or take your kids out for a movie because you need to complete certain pending tasks. It's ok to sacrifice your personal life to a certain extent. You need to make your family understand that whatever it is you're doing, you're doing in the best interest of yourself as well as your family members. Keep remind yourself that you're making these sacrifices now so that the future can be beautiful and smooth.

Sleep: Now we aren't saying that you sleep only 2 or 3 hours a night but you will definitely need to sacrifice on a certain amount of your sleep to start accomplishing your goals. There maybe nights you need to stay up till really late in order to complete pending tasks. It's ok to sleep a little less every now and then to complete your work. But whatever you do ensure that you get at least 5-6 hours of sleep every night irrespective of how busy you are.

Health: During the initial stages of achieving your dreams and goals and breaking out of the rut of poverty, you may end up sacrificing a little bit of your health. Your long work hours may result in a poor diet and limited exercise. This may cause you a little bit of discomfort and inconvenience. In the long run, however, once things are a little settled ensure that you bring your health back to normal and start your exercises again.

Peace: Trying to make your dreams materialize and attempting to accomplish your goals often means sacrificing peace and quiet. Your day becomes so packed with activities and pending tasks that you're constantly on the run. You may not get that time to just sit idle in the evening or catch your breath. Remind yourself that this is only a temporary discomfort and eventually things will come back to normal.

Sanity: Yes, accomplishing your goals can often make you temporarily insane. You're so stressed out and anxious to finish pending work and tasks that sometimes you may feel like you're losing your mind. You may find yourself questioning whether or not what you're doing is actually worth it. It is. Keep going. You will find a light at the end of the tunnel, just don't end up stopping and motivate yourself to keep going forward until you have accomplished your goals.

Desires: There are days when you will feel like you just don't feel like working and would rather indulge in a day of retail therapy or just take the day off and go to a spa. It's times like this that you need to remind yourself that sacrificing such desires right now and focusing on accomplishing your goals instead will make you the rich man or woman you have always wanted to be. So make these basic and temporary sacrifices and continue on the road that leads you to your final destination.

The rich are constantly making such sacrifices in order to get closer to their final goals and accomplish their dreams. They are ready to make certain changes in their lifestyles and you too should start doing the same. As Eric Thomas once said, "To be able at any moment sacrifice what you are for what you will become."

Conclusion:

Your Millionaire Mind

Now that you know it is possible for you to shift your financial energies from negative to positive, it's time you shifted your mindset too. You need to start thinking and behaving like the rich and lose that poor mindset. You need to keep reminding yourself that before anything else, you need to maintain a rich mindset in order for things to work in a positive manner. So now let's briefly go over what it is you need to do in order maintain a rich mindset.

- Have gratitude for all the positive things in your life no matter how big or small they maybe

- Start forgiving people and letting go. There's no need for you to hold on to any kind of negative emotions

- Congratulate people when they are victorious

- Accept your failures with humility

- Give people genuine compliments regularly

- Make sure you read on a daily basis

- Maintain a journal or a diary

- Discuss your ideas openly with those around you

- Maintain a to-do list

- Be open to change

- Set goals and follow them

Once you have decided to change your mindset from the poor to the rich mindset, your next step is to stop pretending. The poor are always pretending like they are rich and purchasing items they don't need just to flaunt them to the world they don't care about. Stop this pretentious act as soon as possible. You don't need to max out your credit card buying products that you can't afford just to impress society. You also need to stop investing all your money in depreciating assets like cars if you really want to break out of your financial mess. If you really wish to live like the rich, the first thing you need to do is stop spending money on things you want and only invest in things you need. Instead of purchasing depreciating assets, invest your funds in appreciating assets like land or gold. Investments in appreciating assets will gradually build your net worth and make you richer.

Your next step to becoming rich is to break out of the rat race. Most people who are struggling with their financial positions have jobs. They barely make ends meet every month and never have enough money left for savings. Their ultimate goal is to keep ascending the corporate ladder and get a bigger job position at their workplace. What they don't realize is that if they need to stop focusing on other people's businesses and consider setting up their very own business. This doesn't mean that they need to quit their job all at once to set up their own business. They can gradually start an online business or a business that they do from their homes in their spare time. They can gradually break out of the rat race and start taking calculated risks. Another thing that the poor don't understand is the power of passive income. The rich on the other hand take passive income very seriously. Passive income is an income that is received regularly with minimal efforts or hard work. Some examples of passive income include rent from the property, royalties, and dividend from stocks etc. So break out of the rat race and also understand the power of passive income and find a way to bring home your passive income.

The next thing that you need to keep in mind is that you need to stop living pay check to pay check if you wish to become rich. If you continue with this pattern, you will never ever become rich. Most of your monthly income will be used up for paying bills and expenses. The chances of you making any savings are slim. If you really want to become rich you need to be willing to break out of your comfort zone and start taking chances. You need to have the courage to take financial risks that are calculated. You need to lose your fear of failure. Failure is the stepping stone to success. The rich are not afraid to fail, on the contrary, they are more afraid to not try. So go ahead and take a few calculated risks if you really want to move forward in life and switch your financial energies from negative to positive.

Another thing you need to keep in mind if you wish to become rich is that you need to stop working for money and start making money work for you. Most people work hard with the intention of making money. Even if you worked 24 hours a day, you would still never make enough money to live the kind of life you dream of. If you really want to live like the rich, start getting your money to work for you. Invest your funds in appreciating assets that make you money, even while you sleep. You can invest your funds in the stock market, in high yielding savings accounts, in real estate, gold, and other such assets. These assets appreciate even while you're sleeping and can really increase your net worth over a period of time. So stop wasting all your time working and slogging making money, instead make money work for you.

Another way to get rich is to start writing down your goals and ensuring that you follow them through. The rich make it a point to write their goals down and do whatever it takes to accomplish those goals. You need to categorize your goals into small term goals, medium term goals, and long term goals. Writing down your goals makes it easier to accomplish them. They act as a reminder to you, they help you stay on track and focused, they give you some sort of direction in life and thus are very important. If you are going to go about life without any goals and wander around aimlessly, you will never ever be able to become rich and successful. Another thing the rich people do is that they set their goals high. They are not afraid to dream big. Even if people laugh at their goals and objectives the rich don't get demotivated. They continue on the path that they feel is best for them and gradually go about accomplishing their dreams. So you too shouldn't be afraid to dream big. It doesn't matter if family members and friends laugh at your plans, dreams, and objectives. Don't get demotivated with the opinions of others. Continue about on your path without a worry and things will work out for you too and before you know it you will be living like the rich.

One absolutely essential behavioral trait that you need in order to become rich is that you need to invest a decent amount of time in yourself. The rich always make it a point to take out sometime during the course of the day and invest it in themselves. It doesn't matter how busy you are or what your job position is, you have exactly 24 hours a day just like everyone else does and if the rich and successful can find time during the course of the day to invest in themselves, so can you. In this time, you need to focus on meditating, exercising, getting out in nature, volunteering to good causes, eating healthy and doing other things that help in self-improvisation. It is essential that you bring about certain changes in your life and health if you really wish to become rich and successful. So compulsorily put aside a few hours of your day and take that time and invest it only in yourself and towards the betterment of your life.

If you want to gain something, you need to be willing to lose something as well. No one said becoming rich was easy, but if that's what you want, the sacrifices you will make will be worth it. In the initial stages when you're trying to break out of your comfort zone and the false sense of security that is blinding you, you may feel extreme discomfort. You may find it very hard to deal with these changes and might crave for the security of your comfort zone. Don't succumb to old patterns and familiar territory; if you wish to shift the financial energy in your life from negative to positive, you need to make some sacrifices. These sacrifices include time, stability, sanity, sleep, health, personal time and other relevant sacrifices. Every time you wish to just give up remind yourself that these sacrifices you're making are simply temporary and it is not a permanent situation that you're stuck in. Every time you get demotivated or want to succumb to personal desires, remind yourself of the long term goal. If you really wish to live the kind of life the rich live, sacrifices are absolutely essential to get you where you wish to be.

So it doesn't matter what mindset you grew up with. It doesn't make a difference what your parents or family members told you. You, just like anyone else, have it within you to become rich. Don't blame your family members for having instilled these wrong ideas in your mind that you can't dream big or become rich. They themselves were raised that way and that's all they know. Their mind has been conditioned to believe that it is not possible to become rich. So instead of listening to them, start thinking differently and make them also realize that they are wrong. Help them become rich too once you have succeeded. One of the best ways to move forward in life successfully is to take people along with you.

Don't be terrified of setting high goals just like the rich, dream as big as you want; change your mindset from the poor mindset to the rich one. Stop wasting money on things you want and spend money only on things you need. Invest wisely in assets that appreciate and not depreciate. Keep yourself happy internally and externally. Exercise regularly, eat healthy, spend time in nature, meditate, work smartly and stop working for money. Make money work for you, increase your net worth in a gradual way, and build your assets. Get rid of your credit cards and if you must only have credit cards use them only for convenience and not for credit. If you have any pending debts that you need to pay off, set up a systematic plan that will help you gradually pay off all the debts. In order to shift your financial energy from poor to rich, you need to begin with clearing all your old debts.

You only live once, but if you do it right then once is all you need. So let go of all that you were taught about the disparity between the rich and poor. This disparity need not be there if you change your mindset. You can be living the exact dream life that you want, just as much as anyone else. Remember, that being rich is not only about being financially well off. You need to be rich from within. You need to spiritually, emotionally and mentally rich. You cannot have a conservative mind and narrow point of view. You need to stop being judgmental and be more open towards other people's points of view. Life is short and everyone has their very own perspective on life. If you don't agree with somebody perspective, that's ok, but that does not make their perspective wrong. We are all here to play a different and unique role. Your role won't be the same as your husband's, wife's or child's role. Just as you require motivation and encouragement learn to be motivating and encouraging to others too. Life is meant to be lived and lived fully. So live a full and a fulfilling life. Think rich, be rich. Don't ever forget that besides financial and materialistic gains keep reminding yourself that, "You're never rich until you have something that money can't buy."

10 Minute Get-Rich Mindset Cheat Sheet

Get-Rich Mindset Cheat Sheet

1) I am very clear about what I want out of life

❑Hell Yeah! ❑ Maybe ❑ Uhh! No

 2) I know exactly the amount of money I want to earn

❑ Hell Yeah! ❑ Maybe ❑ Uhh! No

3) I am obsessed with success.

❑ Hell Yeah! ❑ Maybe ❑ Uhh! No

4) I believe that I will turn my financial goal into reality.

❑ Hell Yeah! ❑ Maybe ❑ Uhh! No

5) I spare time every day to train my mind for success.

❑ Hell Yeah! ❑ Maybe ❑ Uhh! No

6) I believe in providing value in the lives of people.

❑ Hell Yeah! ❑ Maybe ❑ Uhh! No

7) I take consistent action towards my goal.

❑ Hell Yeah! ❑ Maybe ❑ Uhh! No

8) I have written goals to keep me on track.

❑ Hell Yeah! ❑ Maybe ❑ Uhh! No

9) I believe I deserve all the success in life.

❑ Hell Yeah! ❑ Maybe ❑ Uhh! No

10) I have work ethics of a millionaire.

❑ Hell Yeah! ❑ Maybe ❑ Uhh! No

Scoring

Hell Yeah! You get 1 point. _____

Maybe, you get 2 points. _____

Uhh! No, you get 3 points. _____

This is your Final Score. _____

Scored between 10 to 15 points: Congrats, We have a good news, you are in the right direction towards achieving your personal success. The below techniques will strengthen your beliefs and boost in achieving your goals. Keep fighting and you will be victorious.

Scored between 11 to 24: You are on the right track in some important aspect but lacking in some. Find your weakness and take consistent actions on working towards improvement in those areas.

Scored between 25 to 30: You have either not begun your journey towards personal success or working in the wrong direction. You need to analysis yourself, your goals and work towards them as if your life depends on it. Start working on your principle straight away and you are bound to achieve the success you desire.

I am going to make you a money making machine!! The only thing that separates the rich from the poor is their mindset. Answer the below question. When you have completed these questions you will have a clear idea of what you desire. You are only limited by the limitation of your own mind. Dream Big!

What is the exact amount of money you want to make?

_____

_____

What value would you provide in return? (Remember you have to provide in order to receive)

_____

_____

Set a specific timeline, when do you want the money you desire?

_____

_____

What is that one thing you are passionate about?

_____

_____

Find your options are available in order to achieve your goals?

_____

Design an action plan of how you intend on achieving your goals? Write down what step you will take this very moment to work towards your goal keeping our timeline in mind. (You won't do it tomorrow, stop being lazy and do it right now!)

_____

_____

_____

_____

Combine all the answer from above question and again write them down below. (Writing them down again will validate them and make your desire stronger)

_____

_____

_____

_____

Review these goals every single day. This is not given to you by your boss, your parents, or your friends. This is what you want out of your life and you have to do whatever it takes to achieve it.

Reasons

Every one of us encounter situations wherein we become unfocused, doubtful, deviate from our goals and may eventually end up quitting. Writing done 5 reason will bind you to achieve the goals you desire.

It could be to quit your boring job, travel the world, build a business, or buy a fucking Lamborghini! This will provide you the motivation and vision to keep your ass moving.

Write down 5 reasons why it is a must for you to achieve your goals.

1) _____

2) _____

3) _____

4) _____

5) _____

21 Day Habit Challenge

This is a challenge that will help you to review you goals everyday and make them a part of your life. You are required to show up everyday, review your Goals, Reasons and write that you working on them and getting closer day by day.

DAY 1 _____

DAY 2 _____

DAY 3 _____

DAY 4 _____

DAY 5 _____

DAY 6 _____

DAY 7 _____

DAY 8 _____

DAY 9 _____

DAY 10 _____

DAY 11 _____

DAY 12 _____

DAY 13 _____

DAY 14 _____

DAY 15 _____

DAY 16_____

DAY 17_____

DAY 18_____

DAY 19_____

DAY 20_____

DAY 21_____

NOTES: *Write down your daily progress, Ideas, Goals etc.*

NOTES

NOTES

NOTES

NOTES

NOTES

NOTES

NOTES

www.ingramcontent.com/pod-product-compliance
Lightning Source LLC
Chambersburg PA
CBHW070404190526
45169CB00003B/1106